RECESSION PROOF GRADUATE

How to Land The Job You Want By Doing Free Work

Copyright © 2015 Charlie Hoehn

All Rights Reserved

ISBN: 978-0-990-35481-9

1

MY STORY

From first grade to my senior year of college, my record remained virtually flawless.

My overall GPA was 3.8. My SAT and ACT scores were high, I was on the honor roll, belonged to several clubs, etc. I was a cookie-cutter student that counselors tried to mold their students into.

And while I was truly sad that the most fun years of my life were coming to a halt, I wasn't too worried. Sure, the economy was bad, but I'd done exactly what everyone told me to do. I had a solid academic record, great recommendation letters, and a hungry attitude that employers would swoon over. I was ready for the working world.

Yet there I was, less than three months after graduation, lying on my bathroom floor in my parents' basement. I was on the verge of a breakdown. I'd been turned away or completely ignored by every single company I'd applied to (more than 100) over the course of 12 weeks. I was even rejected by a company I'd done a three-month internship with.

Well, I take that back. Two companies were interested in hiring me.

The first was a staging company. Their only job requirements were: have a pulse, and be a chain smoker. The second company turned out to be a pyramid scheme. Thanks, Craigslist!

What the hell? I thought employers would beat a path to my door just to interview me. I thought I deserved a $40,000/year starting salary at least, especially after doing so well in school. I'd done everything they (i.e. teachers, counselors, parents, society) told me to do. Yet I couldn't even get a response.

Why was this so difficult? Why wasn't I on the path to becoming successful?

WHY WOULDN'T ANYONE HIRE ME?!

All of my friends struggled in this awful job market. We all had college degrees and clean track records. Yet none of us could find any decent job prospects.

Our inboxes were full of emails from our parents, containing job listings from CareerBuilder and Monster that sounded miserable. All the good jobs seemed like they were being snatched up by recently laid off 35-year olds who were desperate and willing to take a cut in pay. Us college grads were left with menial gigs that barely required a pulse.

There was a panicked look in the eyes of my peers, who tried to maintain poise as they carefully recited their plans for the future. We looked to each other search for approval, as though we all secretly wanted to ask: *Am I doing this right? Do you have the answers? Do you know?*

We were all desperately trying to figure out the rest of our lives. And strangely, it felt like time was running out. The clock was ticking, and we were racing to hit the milestones of success:

Internship at 21… "Real job" at 22… Great career by 25… Marriage, house, and kids by 30… First million, travel the world by 35… Change the world by 40…

Then coast until retirement, I guess, where we could finally relax and enjoy life.

"You gotta take what you can get in this market" became the mantra of my peers. I stood in shock as someone who I'd partied with months prior proudly exclaimed that they'd been hired in sales at Verizon, and how excited they were to move up to middle manager in a few months...

What?!

Is this what we'd prepared for during all those years of school?

Did our degrees really count for nothing?

Were we doomed to lame 9-5 jobs and hating our lives right out of college?

Not one professor taught us how to buoy ourselves through a recession. And I had no idea what to do, except linger in unemployment and continue eating Hot Pockets.

* * *

Fast-forward eight months...

I was shell-shocked, realizing for the first time how far I'd come. In less than a year, I'd managed to land work with New York Times bestselling authors, a Hollywood filmmaker, and successful entrepreneurs.

My situation was a little surreal. Venture capitalists and billion-dollar companies approached *me* with job offers. I'd stopped sending out my resume; employers came to me first now. I actually reached a point where I was turning away work.

And the best part was that I was working on projects I actually cared about, with people I wanted to learn from. I was having fun and growing, all while doing work that was typically reserved for people twice my age.

This was not the norm for a 22-year old in the heart of a recession.

What separated me from all the other unemployed graduates, sitting in their parents' basement with no job prospects on the horizon?

How was I different from the graduates who had jobs, but already hated their careers?

Well, the truth is that anyone can do what I did. I'm not special or unique, and none of the paid gigs I landed were given to me. I worked hard to earn these dream jobs, but I also avoided the mistakes that most people make.

The one thing that truly separates me from everyone else is that I know something most people don't…

The economy is NOT preventing you from creating your dream career. What's actually holding you back are conventional job-hunting methods. I took all the traditional advice I'd been given and ignored it. I decided to do things differently, and it paid off.

As you're about to see, everyone is doing it all wrong. But I have a method that works.

* * *

What does it mean to be a Recession-Proof Graduate?

- ➤ The economy won't dictate what kind of job you think you can have.

- ➤ You aren't forced into soul-sucking work that causes you to hate your life in your early 20's.

- ➤ You can work with people who are a lot smarter than you and actually continue learning and growing.

- ➤ You can work on projects that you truly care about.

- ➤ You'll have greater control over what type of lifestyle you ultimately want to create for yourself.

Sound good?

I'm going to show you how to make yourself recession-proof. If you successfully apply the principles in this book, you'll be presented with more opportunities than you ever thought possible.

WARNING: NEW RULES

> *"It is not the strongest of the species that survives, nor the most intelligent that survives. It is the one that is most adaptable to change."* – **Charles Darwin**

The principles in this book are... uncommon. None of the courses I took in college taught me how to proactively create my career, so I had to figure this stuff out as I went along. Before we continue, I want to make something very clear:

DON'T expect anyone else to understand these new rules for job hunting.

Your family and friends probably won't understand what you're doing, and they will likely say that you should stick with the old methods (e.g. blasting out your resume to dozens of companies you couldn't care less about). They'll offer outdated advice to you because *that's what they did*, and it's all they know.

You can listen to them if you want, but don't be surprised when you're working in a job you don't care about two years later. Such is the risk of following the crowd.

Consider yourself warned!

3

LIFE AFTER SCHOOL

Most people do absolutely nothing during that first month after graduation. They want a break from their four years of higher education, so they decide to enjoy some time off. A few of them spend several months lounging around.

Some graduates decide to go back to school, which can be a one of the dumbest financial decisions you can make in the United States. A lot of these folks take on massive debt, even though their earning potential will never rise significantly enough to justify it.[1] Two years of lost opportunities and $100,000+ down the drain. Most people considering grad school would be far better off *reading books*, then practicing all the things they learn.[2]

---

[1] Seriously, do the math. Unless you attend an Ivy League school, it's going to take the rest of your adult life to pay off that debt.

[2] The cost of reading a bunch of great books is a few weeks of your time and a couple hundred bucks on Amazon (or free at the library). The investment, however, is priceless. Check out personalmba.com to find the best business books you should read.

A small but growing numbers of graduates try to start their own companies. This is great if you have business savvy and emotional fortitude, but not everyone wants to be an entrepreneur.

Still, other people travel after they're done with school. This can lead to some life-changing experiences and a whole lot of fun. But most graduates are broke; they're worried about bills and have a tough time justifying expensive trips.

Whatever the case… We all eventually become painfully aware that we're unemployed and broke. And that's when the job hunt begins.

So, where does one find a job? More importantly, where does one find a *good job*?

"Um, it's a recession. There are no good jobs, LOL."

Actually, there *are* good jobs. In fact, there will *always* be good jobs. You're just looking in the wrong places. And stop saying "LOL." You deserve to be unemployed when you talk like a 13-year old girl.

As I was saying… Career Builder, Monster, and Craigslist are the sites most graduates use to search for jobs. And, what a shock, none of the job listings sound very appealing.

That's because these three sites are where mediocrity thrives.

Anyone who expects amazing career opportunities from these websites is an idiot (admittedly, I was one of these idiots for a few weeks).

A lot of boring companies successfully lure foolish graduates into applying for lame jobs because it seems like there's nothing better out there.

But the truth is that these sites have mediocre listings by default. Any halfway decent job listing will result in that company receiving *hundreds* of resumes in a matter of hours. Even bad listings consistently get dozens of applications. The competition is outrageous, which makes landing a great gig through these channels almost statistically impossible.[3]

And because your resume looks like everyone else's (white paper, portrait layout, Times New Roman 12-point font), you better have some insanely great credentials on yours if you don't want to be overlooked.

But you won't because you're just another college grad!

Not only are you battling against all the other college grads whose "skills" and "experience" are virtually identical to yours, you're also competing against older people who are willing to take a cut in pay and have 10+ years of experience.

---

[3] Big companies use software to automatically sort through the pile of resumes they receive each week. Resumes that don't contain certain keywords (such as "Harvard" or "MBA") get filtered out, which means the majority of applicants are never even considered.

You're not going to win if you play this game.

Do you see all of the problems with this situation? You are competing against *everyone*, for a limited number of jobs… that no one really wants. Hmm…

These job-listing sites are like city bars. There are typically only a few really hot "offers" in the huge crowd, while the rest are fairly lackluster. And no matter which one you're looking at, there are a bunch of other guys with Ed Hardy shirts fighting for them. This awful "numbers game" is exhausting, so you need a better strategy.

And then you remember: *You have friends!*

Yes, your group of friends (i.e. your network) is one of the quickest and easiest routes for landing a job. In fact, this is the best strategy for getting a job *with the least amount of effort* on your part. If you really need to get a job right out of college, just ask everyone in your network until you find something. Seriously.

Not only do the people in your network already know, like, and trust you (unlike job posting sites where you're just another faceless resume), they will actually *want* to help you find something that's a good fit for you. That makes the job-hunting game much simpler:

Decide what kind of work you're most interested in, and TELL PEOPLE.

Ask your parents to talk to their friends. Ask your friends to talk to their parents. Talk to them face-to-face (don't rely solely on email!), and follow up with them on a regular basis to see if they've heard of anything interesting. I guarantee you that someone knows somebody who's looking for extra help, *even in this economy*.

Now you know how to find a job with little effort on your part. But **you're still left with a glaring problem: finding work that you actually care about.**

Sometimes our network can present us with awesome opportunities, but that's not always the case. The real question is: how do you find work that's intellectually challenging and spiritually sustainable? **How do you create a career that's fun, fulfilling, and financially rewarding?**

I'd like to believe that *all of us* want to work on things we genuinely love and care about. We all want to live a satisfying life that isn't compromised by a job we hate.

We all want to wake up excited for what we're about to work on, and drift to sleep with a sense of joy and happiness… right?[4]

---

[4] Don't want to read the rest of this book? Prefer to watch video instead? No problem. Just visit: learn.charliehoehn.com/rpg

4

THE NEW WAY TO WORK

Pay close attention here, because I'm about to mess you up with the truth.

In terms of rapidly advancing your career and doing work that you actually care about, there is one option that stands above the rest. That option is… **FREE WORK.**

You might be thinking, "I've done free work. It's called an internship, guy. That's no secret."

Well… not quite.

An internship is usually just a menial job without pay.

You have to apply for an internship, the same way you apply for a job. You send in your resume, do an in-person interview, and if you beat all the other applicants, you're given low-level work from 9:00a-5:00p. Enjoy grabbing coffee and filling out spreadsheets for the next three months, sucker. And by the way, there are no guarantees for a full-time position after the internship ends. So all the mind-numbing work you do might not lead to anything. Sorry!

Free work is a different approach altogether…

Free work allows you to work in whatever industry you want, on any projects you're interested in. But unlike an internship, there are no dead ends. If you follow the steps I lay out in the next section, you will be greeted with more opportunities than you ever would have through the traditional career approach.

While free work is great, and can quickly advance your career, there's another component to this equation. **In the beginning, your free work should be done *virtually* (a.k.a. remotely), so you can work with people who live in other parts of the country/world.**

There are many reasons why this is a good idea, but the most important is that it removes nearly all of the perceived risks for the potential employer.

Employers worry about wasting their time and money whenever they hire someone. With free work, you obviously remove the risk of money, but with *virtual* free work, you remove the risk of wasting their time.

If you're not in the same office as them, they don't have to spend a lot of time training and managing you – they don't really even have to think about you. And if you actually do quality work and stick with them long enough, they'll want to continue working with you (and, eventually, hire you).

There's something extremely remarkable about a person who can consistently and quickly complete projects on their own, when they're in another state/country, without the looming pressure of a boss a few feet away.

From a psychological standpoint, free work is extremely powerful. This is because the employer's expectations are always going to be really low:

> **Unproven college grad**
>
> **Working remotely**
>
> + **Zero pay**
> _____
>
> **REALLY low expectations**

If you don't deliver, they will not be surprised or upset -- they almost expect it to happen.

You can use this dynamic to your advantage and dominate.

Don't believe me? Consider this...

Businessmen are *delighted* when they outsource mindless tasks to virtual assistants overseas, at a few bucks an hour, and receive the completed work a few days later.

Now imagine the impact you can have if you do really high quality work, for absolutely free, on valuable projects that require a creative flair.

Your prospective employer will be beyond ecstatic. You will seem like a golden god, and they will praise you for rescuing them from the sea of mediocre job seekers.

Free work is also far better for establishing trust and building healthy working relationships.

Think about it. If you approach an employer with the expectation of a high-paying gig, they will be more cautious and approach the situation as a clear-cut business transaction. If you land the gig, they'll probably get you to sign a contract, maybe even a non-disclosure agreement.

And suddenly there's all this pressure and the expectation that you will deliver greatness. Your employer becomes highly critical of you because you're working on their dime, and they expect you to be a good committed employee.

In other words: You're no longer in control; they are. Lame.

The goal of free work is not so much to become friends with the person (although that can happen), but **to build a healthy relationship and earn their trust.** It's really hard to do that if you're asking them to put you on payroll right away.

Virtual free work also allows you to work in an environment you're comfortable with, so you can stay focused on producing quality work.

When you do free work remotely, you communicate with the person you're working for via email and the occasional phone call. Then you're given free reign to work at your leisure.

You don't have to wake up at 6:00 AM. You don't have to eat lunch in a suit. You can work in whatever environment you're most comfortable in. The only thing your prospective employer wants is for you to do the work you say you're going to do.

Finally, virtual free work enables you to work as much (or as little) as you want.

You can mitigate your risk by doing virtual free work for several clients, instead of just one or two. And trust me: you'll want to work with a handful of clients. One of them may not work out, but most will pay off if you stick with them long enough. Plus, if you realize that one of the arrangements isn't a good fit, you can walk away. No contracts broken, no money lost, and you're right back where you started.

Just be careful when you think about virtual free work in terms of how easy it is to walk away.

In my experience, most people flare out after one task or a single week's worth of free work. They lose interest, fail to see the long-term benefits of developing relationships, or they just feel safer applying for low-paying jobs.

The goal of free work, though, is NOT to be making money immediately. At this point, you're just trying to build a foundation that will justify you making a lot of money *over the course of your entire career,* all while crafting the lifestyle you desire. Understand that it can take time to build that foundation. Even if you aren't making much money right away, you will eventually.

COMMON OBJECTIONS TO FREE WORK

OBJECTION: "It's illegal for employers to accept free work. They must pay at least minimum wage for any work you perform."

With the exception of non-profits, the Department of Labor requires that unpaid work be primarily for the benefit of the *volunteer*, not the employer. YOU are the one initiating this free work arrangement (thus determining the benefits you'll derive), so any complaints you direct to the Department of

Labor will be readily laughed at and dismissed.

People have utilized free work for centuries (see: apprenticeships) as a means to gain incredible experience, sharpen their skills, and learn directly from master craftsmen. Within one year of doing free work, I was able to learn and accomplish more than what I would have achieved in five years of corporate ladder climbing. The experience and relationships I gained were priceless, and they've paid off far more than the scant amount of money I lost in the short-run.

OBJECTION: "I won't be making any money? Is this a joke?"

You will be making money eventually; it's just not going to happen *right away*. There's an important reason for this.

You need to honestly assess whether you enjoy the process of your work or not. If you start with money as the goal, your standards will drop, and you'll be more accepting of poor work conditions.

I've found that I am not totally honest about what I really want when a paycheck is dangled in front of me. I get greedy, rationalizing that I will find a way to enjoy the work that comes with it, and then find myself in an arrangement I can barely tolerate. Free work forces you to assess the quality and fulfillment of the work as objectively as possible, before you make a long-term commitment.

OBJECTION: "But I need to make money!"

You can! While you're developing your unique set of marketable skills, you can find paid work opportunities that employ the use of those skills. Here were a few of the ways I made money while I was doing free work:

- Video shooting and editing
- Podcast editing
- Web and graphic design
- Online marketing consulting
- Selling clothes and old electronics on eBay

Did I make a ton of money? Nope. I made just enough to get by while doing the work I cared about. That's all I really needed at the time.

For some reason, we delude ourselves into thinking we must first go through a year or two of working in a job we hate before we can magically catapult ourselves into the work that we really want to do… *someday*.

But that's not how life works. *Someday* never comes because you didn't start with the work itself; you started with money. Instead of fulfilling your fantasy of transitioning to the work you want to do, you find yourself buying more and more things, paying bigger bills, and trying to keep up with your social circle.

Over time, your purchases and financial obligations look more and more like a cage that you've trapped yourself in. Then one day, you're afraid of leaving that cage behind. So you decide to keep doing the work you hate, just so you can keep paying the bills and making your cage better.

You need to focus on discovering the work you love *right now*. If you have to sacrifice money or work late nights for a little while, go for it. The goal is to become a self-reliant professional who has complete control of how much they earn. When you reach that point, you won't have to worry so much about those bills.

OBJECTION: "It's unethical to do work that you're not getting paid for. It's exploitation, and it degrades your profession."

What if I said you could earn a million dollars playing your favorite sport? Would you be willing to work for free to reach that point? Because nearly every professional athlete was required to work for free in the NCAA first.

Ironically, when an athlete wants to leave college early so they can play professionally, for millions of dollars, people get *upset*. They argue that the athletes are missing out on all of the benefits of free work: valuable experience, skill development, an education, love of the game, etc. Colleges are so sure of the advantages of playing for free that they've created rules to prevent players from moving to paid work too quickly.[5]

Yet for any industry apart from sports, people will readily say that free work is a rip-off. That you're being taken advantage of, wasting your time, hurting the industry, and that your efforts won't lead to anything. And this is when there's just a few thousand dollars at stake!

There are many benefits to free work that make it worth temporarily passing up a paycheck. You get access to unbelievable opportunities, you can work with people who are far above your level, you're challenged with incredible learning experiences, and you discover the work that's

---

[5] Colleges make a ton of money through their sports teams. If they let their best (unpaid) athletes turn pro too fast, then the teams will become less likely to win championships. This ultimately reduces annual revenues via ticket sales, food and beverage, merchandise, sponsorships, etc. It's far more profitable to keep talented players locked in and have them serve their unpaid time for the school.

meaningful and intrinsically rewarding. Most importantly, free work forces you to be honest about how much you actually enjoy the work. Is it fun and fulfilling, or not?

And let's be honest: if you are doing work just for a paycheck – not because you love it or want to do amazing work – then it is YOU who is degrading your profession. It's YOU who is being exploited.

OBJECTION: "Working for free is for suckers. End of story."

How do you feel about your two decades of schoolwork? How's your bank account full of letter grades and gold stars? What have you purchased with your report cards, SAT scores, and degrees?

Surprise! You've been working for free your whole life. All these years, you've been following other people's rules, playing their games. Is it so hard to believe that you have permission to start making up your own rules, and to start playing your own games?

"Find what turns you on. Find what you have a passion for... I had a professor, Ben Graham, I offered to go to work for him for nothing. He said, "You're overpriced." Nonetheless, I went into the business. I will guarantee, you will do well at whatever turns you on. There's no question about that. Don't let anybody else tell you what to do. You figure out what you are doing."

– Warren Buffett (Net worth: $54 Billion). CEO of Berkshire Hathaway, most successful investor of the 20th century.

OBJECTION: "I'd never do free work. I'm not lazy; I just have too much self-respect."

Here's the deal: I'd rather get paid than not make money. But I'd also rather work on stuff I love *for free* than to not do it at all. I make money most of the time, but sometimes, when I really want to do something and know it will be hard to get paid immediately, I'll offer to do it for free.

And you might be shocked to discover: I've met several millionaires, and one billionaire, who openly admit that they do free work on a regular basis. They occasionally work for free, because it leads to hugely lucrative deals, or they just want to do it. And amazingly, these people still manage to keep their self-respect.

OBJECTION: "If you give it to them for free, they are going to expect it to be free forever."

Have you ever downloaded a free app that prompted you to upgrade to the paid version? Maybe you got to use it a few times, or you could only complete a certain number of levels, and then your free trial abruptly came to an end. The app stopped functioning and told you it was time to pay up.

Free work is the exact same concept. It's just a tactic for you to get your foot in the door. Neither you or the employer wants to commit to a formal arrangement yet – you both want to get a feel for what this could be like if you upgraded. If the free trial period is excellent, your employer will conclude that paying you is worth it.

OBJECTION: "No loyalty with free work."

There is a kernel of truth to this. Some people view free work as an easy way to flake out on employers, cutting-and-running at their whim. It's tough to control this dynamic, because free work has to be *intrinsically motivated* in order for it to work. It should go without saying, but you should never propose a free work arrangement that you're not willing to commit to and see through to completion.

But let's not overlook the so-called loyalty that comes with a steady paycheck. A lot of people remain in jobs that they hate simply because they fear losing their income. They don't love the work; they just go through the motions. That's not loyalty; that's holding out.

OBJECTION: "My god... Companies will fire employees and replace them with free workers!"

Free workers are not actively trying to displace anyone; they're trying to create their own positions. But if a free worker happens to be a superior worker than an existing employee with the same responsibilities, then yes, there is a chance that the paid worker will be replaced. Welcome to capitalism!

Free work isn't just for people trying to get hired; employees can also reap the benefits. From reader K. Swanson:

> "I was a teacher for a local school district, and then I started doing free work for the curriculum office. Now I'm heading up lots of special education professional development

projects for the entire county in which I live (and yes, I am getting paid for it!) I truly have my dream job, and I got it by building my portfolio via free work."

OBJECTION: "You're just helping other people get rich! For free!"

Yep. And by working with successful entrepreneurs, I also got to learn how to build wealth for myself.

The issue I had with starting my own business in the past was spending my own money. I didn't know how to spend it wisely, and I was afraid of losing what little I had. I wanted to practice being an entrepreneur so I could build up confidence in my ability to create wealth. That meant helping successful entrepreneurs get richer first, so I could learn on their dime.

Free work allowed me to become an expert. I now have skills and wisdom most people will never develop, which I can use to build wealth for the rest of my life.

OBJECTION: "Free work hurts the economy. If no one is earning, then no one is spending.

Guess what happens when you invest, rather than spend? In a few years, the returns are compounded, and you become *wealthier*. Free work is an investment in <u>you</u>. You are working toward becoming a professional who *creates value* and offers new channels for people to funnel money into. And as more people decide to invest in themselves, our world changes.

Entrepreneurs, artists, inventors, and makers are the ones who create value in our economy. They enrich everyone else's lives by opening up new jobs and businesses that solve our problems and make the world a better place to live. Free work allows us to maximize the results of our most successful creators, while directly passing along their skills and wisdom to the next generation of workers.

The short-term halt on spending pays off over the long run, as the caliber of our creators is collectively raised, and more wealth is ultimately unleashed.

OBJECTION: "I've done free work in exchange for learning and I didn't gain anything from the arrangement. It was a waste of time."

Usually, when you design your own free work program, with specific goals on what you intend to gain from the experience, you'll walk away from the arrangement happy.

Nevertheless, some people have bad experiences doing free work. They're never handed the reins on fulfilling projects, or (in rare instances) they're completely taken for a ride and left with no quality experiences, skills, or contacts to show for all their hard work.

That's why I recommend doing free work *for more than one person*. In the first year, I was doing free work for four people at the same time. I was also juggling a number of paid clients so I could pay my bills and save up some money.

Never put all of your eggs in one basket, especially when your career is just starting out. You need to mitigate against the risk of one of your choices for free work not panning out. Mistakes will be made along the way, so plan for them and quickly move on whenever they arise.

OBJECTION: "There are faster and better ways to earn a living."

There are faster ways to *make money*. But from what I've witnessed, free work is the most effective way to control the course of your career, and ultimately earn a great living.

There are definitely major trade-offs that come with doing

free work. Sometimes it can feel extremely risky or downright awful. For instance, an arrangement might suddenly fall through while you have no money coming in, or your dream clients are consistently ignoring your requests to work together. But every choice in life requires compromise, and the upside to free work is far greater than the conventional job-hunting methods.

Truthfully, I worked harder than most people would have been willing to. I also made a ton of mistakes along the way, and could have easily taken several different paths that would have been immediately more lucrative, but ultimately less fulfilling. There is no *right way* when it comes to your career; there is only *what's right for you*. You might not make much money initially, but you should always be striving to live life on your terms.

> *"I used to drive like 50 miles from Jackson's Point every night to do a set at Yuck Yucks for free. No pay. Not even a gas stub or anything. Nothing. I did that for the longest time, and just kept working until people started to take notice. And the rest is history."*
>
> **— Jim Carrey (Net worth: $150 million).** Award-winning actor, comedian, producer, and one of the biggest stars in Hollywood.

OBJECTION: "Don't young people have it hard enough as it is?"

Stop. The more young people are pitied and coddled, the worse it makes the situation for everyone. We don't need Baby Boomers protecting Millenials from the hardships of life; we need them to encourage young people to become functional adults who can rely on themselves.

One of the main reasons young people have it hard is because we were all encouraged to pursue the exact same credentials within the exact same system. We are all replaceable, and very few graduates have developed the true competitive advantages that employers look for when hiring (such as relevant experience, in-demand skills, and intrinsic motivation).

Things will only get worse for young people if they keep pursuing outdated advice that's been handed down for the past few generations. The last thing we need is to be called back to the old way of work. That way is rapidly fading.

Now, let's get to the fun part. Throw away your resume because you won't need it anymore. I'm going to teach you how to make yourself recession-proof.

Step 0

STOP ACTING ENTITLED

This is step zero, because it shouldn't be a step at all.

Most graduates assume they deserve a big paycheck simply because they have a college degree. They feel as though they are worthy of a great, high-paying job the second they throw their graduation cap into the air. Perhaps it's because we're used to getting trophies just for showing up. Or maybe it's because we spent a lot of time and money working toward a degree, with the implied promise of a "better future."

Whatever the case, this entitlement mentality is toxic. We are not all winners, and we don't deserve to be treated as such simply for existing. Great careers and big paychecks require work. They won't be handed to you.

College degrees are not given to unique snowflake children. They're given to people *who can afford them* (generally speaking), and those who can test well over the course of four years. You may have earned your college degree, but you haven't earned the right to be paid a lot of money (yet).

CASE STUDY

AMERICAN APPAREL'S MARKETING GENIUS

Ryan Holiday dropped out of college at the age of 19. He left school so he could move to Hollywood to do free work for two of his favorite authors: Tucker Max (*I Hope They Serve Beer in Hell*) and Robert Greene (*The 48 Laws of Power*).

Ryan offered to help them with their books and online marketing efforts (e.g. research, generating press, building Wikipedia pages, creating launch campaigns, etc.), and he turned out to be exceptionally skilled at his job. He was so good that both authors recommended him to Dov Charney, the CEO of American Apparel. Dov made Ryan an offer that he couldn't refuse: a six-figure salary working as the director of marketing for the company.

Within three years of dropping out, Ryan established himself as one of the world's top online marketers. He'd generated millions of dollars in sales for American Apparel, at a fraction of the cost of traditional PR campaigns. He'd also advised several New York Times bestselling authors and multi-platinum musicians. Before he was 26 years old, he'd also written and launched his own bestselling book.

Ryan didn't make money for a long time, but the free work he did after leaving school granted him access to extraordinarily talented and connected people, awesome work opportunities, and invaluable experiences. Eventually, he found himself in the exact position he wanted to be in: doing work he loved, and earning more money than he ever would have on the traditional path he'd left behind.

> *"What's money? A man is a success if he gets up in the morning and goes to bed at night and in between does what he wants."* – **Bob Dylan**

Step 1

PICK A FEW INDUSTRIES THAT INTEREST YOU

A lot of us get out of college and realize that we majored in something we don't really care about. Because we've been labeled with that major, we feel pigeonholed. That doesn't have to be how it works, though.

You *can* sidestep your way into almost any industry if you meet the right people and work with them. And at this stage of your career, you should be open to experimentation. Be willing to check out a few industries, just to see what they're actually like. Who cares whether you majored in those fields or not – you're not committing to anything at this point. You're just testing to see whether the work is actually fun and fulfilling for you.[6]

The bigger challenge, I think, is figuring out what kind of lifestyle you ultimately want to create (Active? Creative? Social?), in addition to what fields you are genuinely

---

[6] Check out PivotPlanet.com to connect with experts who can tell you what their industry is like.

interested in. Those two areas should overlap, because you're probably going to be miserable if they don't.

For example, if you want to be active and healthy, you should avoid desk jobs. If you want low stress, don't sign up to be a cop or soldier. If you want flexible work hours and time off to travel, then you shouldn't go to medical or law school. If you need a steady paycheck and structure in your workday, then you shouldn't be a freelancer or entrepreneur.

Stay true to yourself, and be mercilessly honest about what you really want. If you know the career path you're walking on will eventually squelch your interests, your desired lifestyle, or your ability to have fun... then create a better path for yourself. You only get one life, and you are far too young to succumb to misery.

The older we get, the more responsibilities and financial obligations will drop into our laps. Fight for what you want while you're still in your early 20's, so you can have the lifestyle you'll love when you're in your 30's. Now is the time to start creating the life you desire... before it's too late.

Step 2

DEVELOP IN-DEMAND SKILLS

If the highlight of your skill set on your resume is "Proficient in Microsoft Office," then you have no marketable skills. Knowing how to create a document, format a PowerPoint, or organize a spreadsheet are not things you can brag about – those are things every employer expects, like knowing how to pronounce your own name, or remaining continent during office hours.

You need to have actual skills that are both *in high demand* (in your desired industry) and *difficult to learn*. **You'll be extremely valuable if your skill is both scarce and in high demand.**

Seriously, if you want to be making $100,000+ right after college, go learn how to put out oil fires in the Middle East.

Is it miserable and terrifying? Yes.

Is it a skill that's rare and in high demand? Absolutely.

More realistically, iPhone app developers are cleaning up right now because it's a relatively young industry with a strong demand for coders who know how to create quality mobile apps.

Is mobile coding difficult to learn? Sure.

Is it a highly valued skill right now that will lead to multiple offers? Indeed.

You don't have to be an expert in one particular area – you just have to get really good at a few things. When I graduated, I wasn't an "expert" in video editing, or web design, or online marketing, but I was pretty solid at all three. Luckily, they were complementary skills that companies valued as a package deal. I was more marketable because I was good at a few things that were in high demand and difficult to learn (relatively scarce).

Think in terms of what skills your desired industry values, and then start your learning.

You can teach yourself new skills with books, YouTube tutorials, online courses, personal training, and hands-on experience. You can even find someone who has your desired skill set already and beg to shadow them at work (this is how I learned Photoshop for free).

Workers with in-demand skills are what employers really want. That's because skills enable workers to *solve today's* *problems*, which ultimately creates value. Having tons of experience is a bonus, of course, but it's not as important as having in-demand skills.

CASE STUDY

UNOFFICIAL SALESMAN

There's one thing that every business needs in order to survive: **sales**. If you're not sure what in-demand skills you should develop, you can always take on the role of unofficial salesman. That's what Ryan Graves did when he decided he wanted to work for FourSquare.

Ryan went door-to-door to all of the businesses in his neighborhood, demonstrating how the app worked to each of the owners, selling them on the idea of using FourSquare to boost their revenues. With each pitch, his ability to sell the app grew stronger. He knew exactly what business owners needed to hear in order to get on board.

After Ryan signed up more than 20 Chicago venues to run FourSquare specials, he blogged about what he'd done. Then he asked each of those business owners to email the founder of FourSquare with their stories of how he had introduced them to the app. Needless to say, Ryan was hired.

Step 3

BUILD UP YOUR ONLINE SHOWCASE

> *"Great jobs, world-class jobs, jobs people kill for... those jobs don't get filled by people emailing in resumes. Ever."* — **Seth Godin**

"But... But... I don't have *experience*. And no one will hire me, so I can't *get* any experience. No one is giving me a chance. It's so unfair!"

Do you really believe you need to be hired in order to gain experience? Do you honestly think you require an employer's permission before you can get started?

If you're just going to wait around until someone tells you to start working, then good luck! You're going to be waiting for a long time.

You can either pray for great work opportunities to fall in your lap, or you can go out and create them. It's your choice, and it always has been. You can start practicing the work you want to do, right now... or not. You can train yourself in any field that interests you... or not.

Before you decide, let's assess your situation:

You have access to the most powerful resources and creative tools in the history of mankind. You can make movies, *for free*, on your cell phone. You can create a song or an album, *for free*, on your laptop. You can raise thousands of dollars for an art project or business idea, *for free*, on Kickstarter. You can create software, design buildings, automatically invest your money, learn anything you want, and teach people all over the world, *for free*, online. And you can travel to any country *in less than a day*, for just a few hundred dollars.

So… what's stopping you from doing any of these things?
Nearly all of us have access to these same resources. The tool you use to check Facebook is the same tool you can use to edit a documentary, or self-publish a book.

I know countless people who are renowned experts in their fields. They don't have any formal credentials or degrees; they just started teaching themselves, practiced their craft, and shared what they were learning online.

Over time, they gradually built up a fan base that loved their work. A segment of their audience was willing to pay for their products and services. Opportunities to make money grew, and they started turning a portion of those fans into paying customers.

These people didn't wait to be hired; they just went out and created their dream work experience. Eventually, it paid off.

CASE STUDY

HOW TO BECOME A YOUTUBE CELEBRITY

Hollywood: The job market from hell. Being the hub of the entertainment industry makes Los Angeles a more cutthroat city to earn a living in than just about anywhere on the planet. Just ask Taryn Southern.

Taryn moved from Kansas to L.A. at the age of 20, and tried to break into TV hosting for six years. Like most aspiring stars, she struggled to find consistent paid work (all nine of the television pilots she worked on flopped).

After a long series of false starts on other people's projects, she'd finally had enough. Landing the occasional Hollywood deal was no longer a viable career strategy. Instead of waiting for someone to hand her a paycheck and tell her what she could work on, Taryn decided to do the work she wanted to do.

At the end of the day, Taryn really just wanted to make

funny videos. The best place for her to showcase her work was on YouTube, so she changed her focus exclusively to making a great YouTube channel. This free platform allowed her to put out her own videos multiple times per week, as she slowly built her name into a brand.

When she first got started, Taryn was extremely nervous. The quality of her first few videos wasn't great, and a part of her worried that the channel would be a total flop. But she knew that she'd invariably get better at her craft over time, so long as she kept practicing and posting new content.

By the end of the first year, Taryn was making $50 per month from ads displayed on her videos. It wasn't nearly enough to survive in L.A., but the money validated that she was building momentum. She kept putting out new content on her channel, while working an assortment of paid jobs on the side to keep her afloat.

Within two years, Taryn had built up more than 200,000 subscribers on YouTube. The videos she was filming in her bedroom had larger audiences than most cable TV series. Ironically, the networks she'd tried so hard to land deals with years earlier were approaching her with offers for her own shows. Best of all, Taryn was earning enough income from YouTube each month to support her passion full-time.

I've witnessed success stories like Taryn's so many times I've lost count. Believe me when I say: You can do it, too. Maybe not becoming a YouTube celebrity. But creating your dream career? Absolutely.

But first, you have to give yourself permission to get started, to have the courage to put yourself out there and share what you're working on.

Having an online showcase is absolutely essential to your career success. It can also be critical to your survival in the modern world, because of this simple fact:

You will be Googled.

No matter whom you end up working with (or living with, or dating), they will inevitably run a Google search on you and analyze whatever comes up. This can be great if you're in control of your results, but it can be a huge liability if you're not...

If you Googled "Charlie Hoehn" in 2007, you would have seen that two of the top five results were pretty awful. One was a video I submitted to CollegeHumor of my friend drunkenly riding a bicycle down a flight of stairs. The other was from an article in our school newspaper, where I'd been quoted making fun of abortion protestors on our campus.

That's right. "Drunk" and "abortion" were in my top five results. Not good, and far from representative of the man, the patron, the saint...

When you Google my name today, it's mostly rainbows and sunshine.

I was able to bury my bad results with good ones by having a blog (**CharlieHoehn.com**), creating a few social networking accounts (Twitter, LinkedIn, Google Plus), and sharing work that revealed my talents and personality.

There aren't a ton of Charlie Hoehns in the world, so I was able to own the top 10 Google search results for my name pretty easily. It took a few months of work, but it was a great investment of my time.

Unless your name is something like John Smith or Megan Fox, you can usually own your top Google results within a few months. There are a lot of ways to control your personal search results, but my favorite method is blogging.

You can use a blog to write about what you're learning, or jot down your ideas, or post travel pictures, or share videos showing off the latest project you're working on. There are no rules to what you can put on your blog.

But if you decide not to have a blog, you still need to have an online showcase where you can share what you're working on. Whatever platform you decide on should be:

- ✓ Enjoyable and relatively painless for you to use;

- ✓ A social network where like-minded professionals and clients can discover and share your work;

- ✓ Appropriate for your chosen field.

For example… If you're a photographer, you should be posting your photos on Instagram and Flickr. If you're a designer, you should be sharing your work process on Behance. If you're in the entertainment industry, you should be on YouTube or Vimeo. And if you're a professional job applicant, you ought to be on LinkedIn.

No matter what platform you choose, you'll want to have professional quality content coming up whenever someone Googles your name. **Your online content establishes *trust and authority* before employers and clients ever talk to you.** In other words, it's the pre-interview that helps them decide whether you're worth hiring.

I've received a lot of paid work offers from people who have read my blog. Many of them have flat-out said "I trust you" the first time I speak with them, and they're willing to pay me a higher rate simply because they already understand my thought process.

Again, I'm not special. You can do the exact same thing. It just takes effort.

HOW TO START YOUR BLOG IN 7 MINUTES

1. **Go to Wordpress.com and click "Sign up now."** Wordpress is the most popular blogging platform on the Web, powering more than 60 million websites.

2. **Register a domain.** You can choose any name for your blog, but I suggest setting your full name as the domain address. To do this, enter your name as the username in the Sign Up process. For instance, if your name is Phil Sampson, set your username to 'philsampson.' This makes your blog's address philsampson.wordpress.com, which you can easily convert to philsampson.com with a $15 payment.

3. **Set up pages to make your blog easy to navigate.** At the very least, you should create an "About" page, a "Contact" page, and an email form where visitors can subscribe to your updates. Play around with the different design templates to modify the look and functionality of your blog.

4. **Start blogging.** You can post about anything you want. The point is to create a website that puts you in a

professional and positive light (unlike your Facebook account, which has pictures of you with your beloved beer bong). If you want to use your blog to get employers interested in you, I suggest you write about things that they'll find valuable and relevant. You can write about your past work experiences, things you're learning about, current projects you're working on, etc. Just be honest and don't over-inflate your accomplishments.

I don't think it's important to post new content every day, or even every week; you just need to make building up your online showcase a regular part of your routine while you're searching for work.

More Blogging Resources

- **Medium (medium.com).** Beautifully simple blog platform that connects people with stories and ideas.

- **Tumblr (tumblr.com).** Follow the blogs you've been hearing about. Share the things you love.

- **Strikingly (strikingly.com).** Set up gorgeous, mobile-friendly websites in minutes.

- **SumoMe (sumome.com).** Tools to grow your blog's traffic and subscribers. Fast and painless set up.

Step 4
PAY BILLS, CUT COSTS

For people who want to pursue the free work route, I recommend working a day job to pay the bills, or finding ways to make a lot of money in sporadic bursts. At the end of the day, you just need to find some means of making enough cash to cover your expenses.

Free work can launch you into your dream career, but as the name implies, you won't be making money from it for a while. You'll need to find one or more sources of income. This is where your in-demand skills come in handy.

Even if you have a boring day job, you can earn extra income on the side by using your skills and resources. For me, I offered entrepreneurs and companies online marketing consulting, web design work, and freelance video/audio editing. You can offer any service people need: babysitting, cooking healthy meals, fitness training, or dog walking. Here are a few more options to consider:

> ➤ **AirBNB (airbnb.com).** The easiest way to monetize your extra space. If you live in a big city, you should absolutely try this. My friend earned $39,000 in eight

weeks, renting out his San Francisco apartment to conference attendees.

➤ **Etsy (etsy.com)**. Sell handmade goods to people around the world.

➤ **Gumroad (gumroad.com).** Sell any digital product you've created in seconds.

➤ **Uber (uber.com**). If you have a car, you can sign up to be a driver and earn money as an independent contractor. Get paid weekly, be your own boss, and get paid in fares for driving on your own schedule.

There are countless ways to earn money (even while you're doing free work), so long as you stay focused on helping people who are able and willing to pay for your help.

As an aside: If you decide to pursue the freelancing route right out of college, then you better brace yourself because it's not easy. You have to cut down on nearly all of your *immaterial* costs because there might be weeks, or sometimes months, where you won't make much money at all. Big clients will unexpectedly bail on you or decide they don't need your help anymore. That can be devastating if you don't have a bunch of other clients lined up. You will have to hustle, make phone calls, and sell people on your services. In other words, you'll need to work hard to stay afloat.

I'm telling you all this because, well, doing free work can be financially straining. It's not easy to see your friends buying multiple rounds of drinks for your whole group at the bar because they're getting a steady paycheck each week. At some point, you will want to quit doing free work and just get a normal job like everyone else.

Ignore that temptation! **When you're young and broke, money is a siren.** It's alluring because you can have it right away if you get a run-of-the-mill, uninteresting 9-5 job. But you'll probably compromise your happiness over the long run.

Doing free work will be tough on your bank account for a brief period, but you'll make huge financial gains in the future while simultaneously advancing your career in the direction you want it to go.

Ultimately, it's your decision. Do you want a steady paycheck at a job you're not crazy about, or are you willing to temporarily postpone money in exchange for amazing learning opportunities that will pay off big in a year or two?

Step 5

PICK YOUR PARTNER

Choosing the right person to do free work for is arguably the most important step in this whole process. They must be someone you'd like to learn from and emulate, who's doing awesome work that you want to be a part of.

Here are some questions you should ask while deciding on your ideal partner:

- ✓ Does this person have a history of quality work and meaningful pursuits that resonates with my values?

- ✓ Would working with this person help me grow into a better version of myself?

- ✓ Will my association with this person have a positive impact on my reputation?

- ✓ Would this person give me access to priceless experiences and amazing people that are currently out of my reach?

✓ Does this person have the financial resources to compensate me fairly if/when we transition to a paid working arrangement?

The biggest thing to keep in mind is that you want to *aim high*. Find people who are seemingly unreachable to a recent college graduate, and go after them.[7]

Because you're a young hustler who's willing to work for free, your qualifications will matter less. You'll have a higher success rate if you approach the "high-hanging fruit" that no other graduates are going after. Less competition means a better chance of you getting work.

In my opinion, a person taking the free work route should try to work for a successful entrepreneur who is still on the upswing. There are many reasons for this.

First of all, entrepreneurs tend to move at a breakneck pace compared to the corporate world. They are not interested in pushing papers; they want to get things done fast and make change happen. They have very clear priorities (validate, sell, grow). Their enthusiasm is contagious, and their work

---

[7] Celebrities and extremely famous people aren't usually ideal partners. Most of them are ridiculously busy, a little insane, and they won't set aside much time to invest in your learning.

ethic is much stronger than your average employee at a big company.

You want to be around successful entrepreneurs as much as you can, because you will begin to absorb their business savvy, optimistic attitude, and strong work ethic. You will not regret the decision to expose yourself to their work process — you'll gain some of their entrepreneurial DNA and make it your own. Even if you don't want to become an entrepreneur yourself, you will still gain a lot from the experience.

Secondly, there are a lot of entrepreneurs but only a small percentage of them are *successful*. When you work with an entrepreneur who has already achieved success and now has their sights set even higher, you'll have a much better chance at being involved in a future success of theirs. Not a bad idea to hitch yourself onto a rising star. But the ones who are unproven are much riskier for you, because they may never succeed. Not only are they too poor to pay you now, there's a fair chance that they will *always* be too poor to pay you.

It's fine to work with a brilliant inventor or a gifted artist, but if they know nothing about sales, or marketing, or raising money, or running a business, they are going to have a really tough time sustaining their hobby. And you will run the risk of never getting paid for your efforts. You need to get your foot in the door with people who already know what they're doing.

CASE STUDY

HOW TO GET HIRED BY STEVE JOBS

Bas Ording was sitting in the lobby of Apple's headquarters, looking bewildered and dejected. The company was searching for a graphical interface designer to help with their new operating system. Unfortunately, Bas was nervous during his meeting with the HR department, and they weren't impressed with how he'd presented himself.

Just as Bas was about to leave, he ran into Steve Jobs in the lobby. Bas quickly opened his laptop, and ran a demo he'd put together using Adobe Director, which showed how Apple could fit more applications in the dock. As his mouse cursor hovered over the applications, the size of the icons increased, as though they were under a magnifying glass. "My God," Jobs said. He hired Bas on the spot.

Bas didn't have to be on Apple's payroll to create his idea. Nor was he afraid of his idea being stolen, because he knew he had even more to offer. He used free work to get his foot in the door, to demonstrate what he was capable of, and prove his value.

No matter what field you're interested in — photography, architecture, cooking, fashion, etc. — the people who are earning the most in that industry are all *successful entrepreneurs.* These people were all able to turn their skills and passions into businesses (automated systems that earn money by solving other people's problems).

Everyone I did free work for was a self-made entrepreneur, because that's what I wanted to become. I was a genuine fan of their work, knew all about their past projects, and researched them extensively to figure out what problems they were facing. Then I came up with ways that I might be able to help them, so they'd want to teach me how they started and ran their business.

So… where does one find successful entrepreneurs?

Think about the products and services that you love and use regularly. Think about all the companies that you buy from repeatedly throughout the year. Entrepreneurs created those businesses. You can do research on them and figure out which ones might be easy to approach and receptive to the idea of free work.

If you're having trouble finding successful entrepreneurs, just look on Amazon. Click on some of the bestsellers in different product categories, and you'll see a bunch of great products being sold by companies you've never heard of. Entrepreneurs built every single one of those companies. Or check out AngelList.co, where you can take a peek at some of the hottest tech startups in the world.

Another great place to find up-and-coming entrepreneurs is on Kickstarter.com.

Kickstarter projects that receive over $100K in funding — or get 200%+ funding — clearly have proven demand. The people who are running these projects are onto something big, and they are likely freaking out about having to fill all those orders. Many of them are under more pressure than they've ever dealt with. The sweet smell of opportunity is in the air…

If you find a project that you love, and the people running it seem intelligent, ethical, and appear to know what they're doing, then you can contact them and offer to help.

But before you reach out, you need to do a ton of research on them. I'll often spend several hours researching a target before I start writing my proposal, just so I can be absolutely certain that our values are aligned and a work arrangement will be harmonious. This is why I tend to choose partners who have an extensive online presence. I can discover so much about their needs just by poring over their Google results.

Ask yourself these questions while researching your ideal partner(s):

- ✓ What are their primary sources of revenue, and how can we leverage them without damaging their brand?

- ✓ What areas of their business are the strongest? How could we enhance those strengths and improve their results with my skill set?

- ✓ What areas of their business appear to be weak, or sources of stress? How can we use my skills to reduce or fix those problems?

- ✓ What challenges are they facing over the next 6-12 months? How can I help them implement practical solutions to overcome those challenges?

- ✓ What are their competitors doing that they are not?

- ✓ What are three products we could make and sell to their customers without damaging their brand?

Your answers will form a list of ways you can help them. Draw a star next to the answers that you believe will be the most valuable for them. Put another star next to the ideas that you're confident you can execute.

CASE STUDY

HOW A MILLIONAIRE DID FREE WORK FOR A BILLION DOLLAR COMPANY

Kevin Rose is one of the most famous entrepreneurs in Silicon Valley. When he was 27 years old, he founded Digg.com, a social news website that allowed users to discover, share, and recommend interesting content. At the height of its popularity, the site attracted more than 236 million annual visitors. Rose quickly became the face of the next wave of journalism: democratized news.

Over the years, Kevin built up an impressive portfolio of tech startups he'd invested in, including Facebook, Twitter, FourSquare, and GoWalla. Because of his success with Digg, he often had early access to invest in the Valley's hottest startups...with the exception of Square.

Square was a brand new mobile payments app, founded by Jack Dorsey (the creator of Twitter). The company offered vendors a free credit card swiping device that could be plugged into the headphone jack of cell phones and tablets. The convenience of Square allowed any individual vendor (restaurants, theaters, cafes, food carts, musicians, etc.) to replace costly and bulky credit card machines with their smart phone.

Kevin fell in love with the idea, and was eager to invest. He knew that if Square succeeded, they would become a multi-billion dollar company. The only problem was that every investor in the Valley wanted in on the deal, and Square's first round of angel investing (known as Series A) was over.

Kevin called up Jack Dorsey and asked if it was still possible for him to invest. Jack politely turned him down, telling him that he'd be first in line for series B. Unfortunately, series B meant spending more money for an investment that would ultimately be worth less. Kevin was frustrated, but still believed he could get in on the ground floor.

He began studying Square's website, and noticed that the company didn't have any demo videos of their product. He quickly went to work, putting together a 2-minute high-definition video trailer that showed how easy Square was to use on an iPhone. He posted the video to his YouTube channel, where it was viewed more than 300,000 times.

Then he sent the link to Jack Dorsey, who was extremely grateful for the demo video and free publicity. After seeing the value Kevin was able to provide for the company, Jack made him an exclusive offer to get in on the Series A round.

At the time Kevin invested in Square, the company was valued at $40 million. Today, Square is worth more than $3.25 billion – a stunning growth of 8,125%. Kevin's decision to do free work for Square resulted in one of his most lucrative investments to date.

Step 6

PITCH FREE WORK

At this point, you have your target picked, you are interested in their work, and you've done your research. You know you can benefit them in a big way... but how should you contact them?

Simple. Just send them an email. Here's a sample pitch:

> **SUBJECT: I want to work for you, for free**
>
> Hi [NAME],
>
> I'm a long-time fan of your work, and I really believe in [DESCRIBE THEIR MISSION]. I have some ideas about how we can further that and make it even easier for you to [INCREASE REVENUE, ETC]. Your work is important, and I believe I can help you get to the next level.
>
> Here's my idea: I would love to [PROJECT YOU CAN COMPLETE REMOTELY], which will ultimately help you [INCREASE SALES / REDUCE COSTS / MAKE CUSTOMERS HAPPIER]. I am an expert in [YOUR IN-DEMAND SKILL SET]. I've worked with [CLIENTS OR COMPANIES YOU'VE

HELPED], and helped them achieve [RESULTS]. Here is a sample of the quality you can expect from me: [LINK TO YOUR ONLINE SHOWCASE, OR SAMPLE OF YOUR WORK]

I don't normally discount my rates, but I'm willing to do this project for free. I'll send you a few brief updates on my progress for the next two weeks. If you don't like my work, you can scrap it and move on (no money lost, and no hard feelings from me). But if you do like my work, I'd love to discuss a few more ideas for helping you with your business, and the potential of a more formal work arrangement.

Would a discussion on how to help you [ADVANCE YOUR MISSION] be of interest? If so, let's set up a call. Does next Tuesday @ 1:30p or 3:00p EST work for you? I can be reached at [PHONE #].

This script is highly effective, and very difficult for employers to turn down. I've had a lot of success with it.

Whatever project you propose should directly benefit the person you're emailing, and conveniently require your skill set. Explicitly lay out how your proposal will improve their efforts, and why they need *your help*.

Make sure to pitch projects that are valuable *in their terms*. Don't just say "Hey there, I've got these skills, you should pay me for them!" Instead, ask yourself: "How can I frame my services in a way that will be super valuable for this person?"

Very few job seekers take the time to actually put themselves in the shoes of prospective employers.

That's why this is such a good way for you to differentiate yourself and stand above the crowd. Even if the employer thinks your ideas are slightly flawed, your proposal will be memorable and hard to turn down.

If they don't respond, don't worry. They're probably very busy and buried in emails, or they might just be wary of your offer. Follow up every 4-7 days with this:

> Hi [NAME],
>
> Just a quick follow up on my previous email...
>
> Would a conversation on how to help [ADVANCE YOUR MISSION] be of interest?

If they're still not responding after a few of these follow ups, either call them or move on to pitching another prospect with your ideas. There are plenty of great entrepreneurs and businesses out there that could use your help. Don't get too upset if one of them isn't interested.

You still might be skeptical, wondering why on earth you should offer free work to an entrepreneur...

Well, a lot of them are doing really cool and meaningful work. I hear people complain all the time about not wanting to work for a soul-sucking, boring corporation.

Entrepreneurs are creative people who build businesses that they're passionate about. Some of them raise a ton of money, but are too busy or inexperienced to pull everything off. Even though they might have a viable business on their hands, they could still be in the early stages where failure is likely.

If only they could find a talented partner to work with…

Why not pinpoint their biggest problems and stumbling blocks, then reach out with an offer to help? If you can actually deliver what you're promising, then they will have a lot more to lose by not keeping you around than you'll have to lose by working for free. They will be happy to pay if you prove you're worth it. They might even offer you significant percentage of the company.

CASE STUDY

HOW A FAN TURNED HIS FAVORITE COMIC INTO AN EMPIRE

Robert Khoo was a huge fan of Penny Arcade, a popular web comic that revolved around video games. The comic built up a loyal readership over the years, but the founders of the company, Mike Krahulik and Jerry Holkins, struggled with running the operations side of the business (they'd accidentally sold off the company twice!)

When Robert found himself in a meeting with the two founders, he quickly realized that – even though they were amazing artists -- they had no idea how to run a company. Opportunity knocked... Robert put together a 50-page business plan for Penny Arcade, then handed his proposal to the founders. He told them:

> Here's the deal: this business plan is yours, no matter what. But I would love to execute it myself. I have the market experience, and I'm a gamer so I definitely understand the space. You give me the green light and I will quit my job and work for you for free for two months. If I can pay for myself after two months,

> great, keep me. And if I can't, cut me.
>
> How could they refuse? Within a few years, Penny Arcade was drawing in 3.5 million readers annually, with revenues believed to be in the low seven-figures. And thanks to his help with making Penny Arcade a financial success, Robert Khoo is now president of the company.

A lot of free workers get to work on projects they love. Take Dave, the Wells Fargo banker who was sick of his 9-5 job. He reached out to a filmmaker on Kickstarter, and offered to work for free as a videographer on their documentary. He traveled around South America for a month, and ended up as a subject in the film. He said it was the best decision he'd ever made in his life.

If you really want to get involved with a unique and meaningful business, Kickstarter is a great place to start. The overall goal is to seek out amazing experiences that steps up your game, develops your in-demand skills, surrounds you with talented people, and teaches you how to create value for others (which allows you to earn money).

Step 7
SWITCH TO <u>PAID</u> WORK

Before you set up a long-term deal, you ought to set a tentative deadline for when the "free work" transitions to "paid work."

If six weeks is your limit, say that you'd like to either transition to paid work by then, or ask them to help you move toward more challenging and lucrative opportunities by referring you to people in their network.

It helps to set these expectations *after* you've done enough great work to gain the person's trust and approval. Otherwise, you'll condition them to expect free work indefinitely. Not good.

Be appreciative at the opportunity they're affording you, but make it clear that you're also in a financially tight spot.

Let them know that, at some point, you'll need to switch to some form of reimbursement for your hard work.

Here's what you can say:

> Hi [NAME],
>
> We've been working together for [NUMBER OF WEEKS] now, and I'm thrilled with everything we've accomplished. Since we first started, we've [RESULTS YOU'VE DRIVEN, IMPACT YOU'VE MADE]. The whole experience has been invaluable to me, and I really appreciate you giving me a fair shot.
>
> My free trial run is coming to an end, but I would love to keep working together. Going forward, I'll continue working on projects that will move you toward your goals and bring your business to the next level. In fact, the next project I'd love to tackle is [ANOTHER IDEA THAT WILL BE VALUABLE]. The only change, of course, is that I would be charging for my services from this point forward.
>
> Are you still interested in working together on a paid basis? Please let me know what you think. Either way, I'm extremely grateful for the opportunity, and I wish you all the best in the future.

Assuming you've done a great job so far, they will want to keep you around. You've proven the value of your work, they trust you, and they know it will be a hassle finding and training someone else who can fill your role (after all, great help is hard to find). Either way, you can add the work experience and their testimonial to your online showcase.

People won't take advantage of you unless you let them.

Be assertive and don't get into a long-term deal with someone unless you're both comfortable with the agreement. If you're reliable and do good work, they'll have more to lose by not paying you then you will by working for free.

WHEN TO SAY NO TO FREE WORK

Free work is a great way to launch your career and move into the job of your dreams. However, there are a number of scenarios where you'll want to avoid doing free work completely. The situations listed below will bring you nothing but lost time and heartbreak. You've been warned!

SCENARIO: They suggest you work for free.

Free work is your proposition, not theirs. Your client can give you projects to work on, but if they're the ones insisting on not paying you, you should probably switch to someone who's not a freeloader. Unless the work is something you would absolutely love to do, you should just move on.

Also, anyone who suggests that you work for free will usually suggest that you keep doing it. This won't be the last time they'll ask you to work without pay.

SCENARIO: They say it's "great exposure."

Unless they're going to repeatedly put your name and work in front of hundreds or thousands of dream clients, "great exposure" pretty much never pans out to anything. Really, it's a joke.

Instead of accepting exposure as payment, ask if they'd be willing to introduce you to a few of their best contacts who would be willing to pay you (offer suggestions of who you have in mind).

SCENARIO: They aggressively try to sell you on this "amazing opportunity."

Desperate people are desperate for a reason. They view you as their only option. And if you're a total beginner and they're trying extremely hard to seduce you, you should run for the hills.

SCENARIO: You're fairly certain you will gain nothing positive from the arrangement.

The purpose of free work is growth, learning, gaining experience, and building relationships with awesome people. If the opportunity doesn't offer any of those things, then you should either not do it at all, or you should be getting well compensated for your time and effort.

SCENARIO: You strongly suspect your client will never be able to pay you.

There's a reason why I advocate working with <u>successful</u> entrepreneurs. Know what you're getting into by looking at your client's track record. If they have a long history of never making any money, then you need to face the facts: you are probably going to be poor with them.

SCENARIO: Your client says they'd rather pay you "a little money" than have you work for free.

Sometimes your client will try to change your free work offer to a low paid arrangement. This is a really bad idea. It's far better for everyone if you work for FREE (at least in the beginning), rather than cheap.

Working for very little pay always damages both sides' perception of the other. You grow to resent them because you're not being paid what you're worth, and they lose respect for you because they've mentally associated your work as "cheap." And that is a very difficult position to get out of.

Politely tell them that you'd hoped to demonstrate your value first, just to see if this could be a good fit for a long-term arrangement. If they're unwilling to compensate you later on for the value you're creating for their business (opting for cheap instead), then just go your separate ways. People who try to get you to sell yourself at a low price aren't worth your time.

SCENARIO: You suspect the work is going to be a nightmare.

If your gut is telling you that that this arrangement is going to be a major pain (e.g. the client is a jerk, the work completely drains you of energy), you need to gracefully make your exit as swiftly as possible. Your time is limited, and there are endless opportunities in this lifetime for you to tackle. Don't waste your life on work that feels like torture.

And if you've already made a long-term commitment, or you're halfway through a major project, DO NOT CUT AND RUN. This is a horrible thing to do to the other person. Instead, take a few days to create your exit strategy. Lay out all the things they currently rely on you to do, and figure out the exact steps they'll need to take in order to replace you in the least amount of time.

"But isn't that the client's responsibility?" Yes, but your reputation is on the line. If you're quitting a free work arrangement that you set up, it's up to YOU to accept responsibility for the position you'll be leaving your client in. A graceful and respectable exit will leave them with a positive impression of you.

Over time, you will develop a reputation that precedes you, and a portfolio that qualifies you as an expert. Your online showcase will become a magnet for opportunities, and you'll be approached with more offers than you can handle.

As demand for your work rises, you will double or triple your rates. You will charge premium pricing so clients value your services even more, or you will strike out on your own to create a business. There may even come a day when someone offers to work for you, for free.

And that is how you become a Recession-Proof Graduate.

NEXT STEPS

If you want step-by-step guidance and support from a community of free workers, check out the **Recession-Proof Graduate VIP Course**. This is the career course you wish you could've taken in school… You'll get access to hours of video lessons, case studies, and priceless interviews with free work success stories. Just visit the link below:

> learn.charliehoehn.com/rpg

Oh, and if you enjoyed this book, would you mind taking a minute to leave a review on Amazon? Even a short review helps, and it would really mean a lot. Many thanks :)

If you want to share your free work story with me, go to:

> charliehoehn.com/contact

"Don't worry… It's a great adventure, your life, and it's only just begun." **– Shantaram**

BOOK CHARLIE TO SPEAK

Charlie Hoehn is a professional speaker. He's delivered keynotes and led workshops at TEDx events, conferences, universities, and companies around the country.

"I felt energized after his speech, as if a rocket had been shoved up my trousers and lit with a match." **- TEDxCMU**

"Charlie has a unique ability to get any type of audience to think outside of the box... It's very rare to find someone who's able to give advice to an audience like they would to their best friend." **- Startup Weekend**

"Boy did he knock it out of the park! His message was spot on and the audience was truly engaged. We hope his schedule will allow him to speak at all of our future events, as well!" **– American Dream U**

For more info, visit **CharlieHoehn.com**

Made in the USA
Columbia, SC
19 March 2024

33330498R00050